Found It

Written by

Aoife Caige

Intro

The seekers, the ones not satisfied with how things are going in their lives are my people. Those simmering pots of anxiety and the intellectuals who feel like pebbles at the bottom of a stream just sitting there. They are not doing anything and are not entirely sure what to do about it.

This book may be for you.

This book may be for you also, if:

- You want to be the best version of yourself, but are not sure how to get there
- You hate everyone, including yourself
- You love everyone, including yourself
- You are stuck and not sure why you are stuck

If you happen to be one of the lucky ones and have all the answers, great! Close this book and donate it to someone.

I want you to be content with yourself.

If after this book, you still have no idea what to do and are still the same as before you read this book, please donate it to someone else. They may benefit from something inside of these pages.

I hope you donate all your self-help books, to be honest. I hope this is the last one you will ever need to read.

You have been tripled dared.

Author's Corner

I have had four name changes. Yep, four. The last one I am sticking with though. The paperwork and absolute pain in the ass of changing everything with your name on it; is getting increasingly strenuous. Two of the three of the name changes were from marriage or divorces and going back to my birth name. I wish it were for something fun or other glamorous reason. I am not a spy, nor am I trying to hide from anyone.

In between all that name swapping, I have lived a thousand lives in this one. I am not the same person I was at forty, thirty, twenty, ten, or even five years ago. Physically, mentally, emotionally, and spiritually; I am not the same as I once was. If you knew me at any time in the last forty-odd years, you may not recognize my outlook today. Who you knew is a past, foreign version of myself. If you liked her, great, she could be all right at times.

I began my search for the perfect religion at age thirteen, was a lead singer in a band, and raised two precious children from my womb. I have read thousands of books. I blame Reading Rainbow for this voracious reading appetite! I have a bachelor's degree in philosophy and a master's degree in business administration. I had a cosmetology licensed in Aesthetics, a Certified Scrum Master, and am a certified yoga teacher.

I have been married, divorced, a girlfriend, a mistress, and a lover. I have been homeless, witless, and completely out of my mind, out of a job, and out of luck. I have lived in a million-dollar home and lived in my car. I have had a near death experience and survived traumas so horrific they bear not be repeated. I have been a terrible person, a great friend, and a jealous asshole.

I have been everything.

Pull up a chair.

:P Aoife E. Caige

Chapter 1.0

The more innocent children seem, the smarter and cleverer they are. Heads up to all you future parents and current ones. Everyone thought I was an angel, which I was, when I wanted to be. Because of my personal history, my sweet babies could barely breathe in the wrong direction without me right there in their business. That was helicopter parenting at its finest. I realize this now, sorry K and P.

Kids should get plenty of fresh air and sunshine. Room to breathe and make a mess are equally important. That is how we learn, by making a mess, by making mistakes. Other GenXrs like myself will nod in appreciation when I tell you that it was not uncommon for me to walk through miles of woods to the banks of the St. Croix River. [i] Explore said woods, play on the riverbanks in the water, climb up a cliff (freehanded), climb up the town's water tower (also freehanded), and then walk back home in time for lunch = at age nine.

Just a regular Saturday.

Right at this very moment Mom and Dad are reading this and had no idea, so, surprise! Probably makes sense as to why I came home so dirty all the time. That aqua water tower paint liked to stay on clothing! [ii] I became skilled at dodging tree limbs and stepping lightly so as to not wake or disturb creatures.

Once I got my ten-speed bike I would bike for miles out of town, on country roads, to parts of the farmland countryside people outside of the adjacent lands, rarely see. Walking through town, at night, up to my boyfriends home, the two-mile trip, in the dark, with no flashlight, knowing exactly when and where to hide when a car came by, where the neighbor fences were, and where the dogs and motion lights were located - was my specialty before I had my driver's license. As an aside: To this day, I can take a group of people in the dark through the woods for miles, and not lose one, or be harmed.

It is a weird flex, but it is mine.

I always felt safe and protected in the wild. It was like someone, or something was watching me, making sure I was ok, but let me run absolutely feral and free. There was no Stop, there was only Go. This deeply rooted sense of safety and security is within everyone. I just happened to have a ton of it in the beginning decade of my life.

"Audaces fortuna iuvat - Fortune favors the bold."
— Virgil[iii]

As I got older the church, societal pressures of the 80s and 90s, other girls, teenagers, adults, boys, boyfriends, fake friends, real friends, and abuse - dampened my sense of wellness and wellbeing. I began to fade. I was still "in there" but had started a type of cocoon to insulate myself from the world. I will be hanging out in there for years to come. When you begin to draw inward and insulate against the harsh words or world, it is never a good sign. This, my friends, is an ancient survival tactic. At the time it feels good. You feel all snuggly in your warm little cocoon. You shut out life and everyone in it. What would you have chosen to do otherwise, right?

Exactly. What does one do when you are in the middle of the emotional freefall that is the majority portion of your life? You fall into a time of unwellness, uneasiness, and unholiness. My cocoon was dark and unhealthy. Years of severe depression, suicidal thoughts, medications, drinking, and trying everything to feel better, just made everything exponentially worse. I tried moving from my hometown, changing religions, changing romantic partners, changing jobs, changing friends, changing my hair color, changing my goals, chasing tail, going no contact, going out every night, having kids, getting married, getting divorced, being a full time mom, being a part time mom, being a bitch, being a sweetheart, being a doormat, travelling, and generally trying to outrun my problems. I was on a roller coaster / Ferris wheel / merry-go-round of emotions, hormones, and drama. I had read every single self-help book on the library shelves of the three large, two sided sections.

Nothing worked.

Strike one.

The Research

In the meantime, I asked everyone I could about how to better my situation, my feelings, and my now loathsome state of being. Everyone including pastors, my parents, my friends, co-workers, strangers on the street, strangers in bars, strangers in line at the grocery store, strangers on planes, friends of friends, enemies, psychics, palm readers, tarot readers (one was fantastic by the way who predicted a few things that happened three years after our reading, RIP B), Hindus, Muslims, Christians, Buddhists, Atheists, Nihilists, Agnostics, and a ton of Skeptics (for some reason they were plentiful).

In between critically exanimating people's answers, I read the great books of major and minor religions. I then moved onto asking Philosophy majors and Philosophy professors. Almost done, readers, hang in there. I read the great philosophers' writings, asked other professors, teachers, old teachers, new teachers, my bosses, my lovers, my kids' babysitters, my kid's daycare (for whom I call their second mother, thank you forever L.B.), people I met on the dancefloor, people at social gatherings of family members, family members themselves (thank you Grammy, RIP), and those who shall remain anonymous.

Everyone gave me different answers to my questions.

AGH!

Strike two.

All were kind, albeit annoyed with the continual peppering of "Why" and "How" questions. If they were successful I would know because I changed one thought to a more successful one. Most times they were listened to intently, but overall dismissed. I was searching for the truth. My truth. What resonates with me, throughout my entire essence, and no one could quite get there. They had pieces, but not the whole puzzle.

The real truth underneath it all was that I could not face myself, or my problems. Asking everyone in hopes that something they said would help make me feel less awful about my life became an addiction, in and of itself. A minority of those helpful peoples' tidbits made their way into my psyche. The rest of it just floated back into the ether. I was not ready to listen, to be honest. I was addicted to research. Fanfuckingtastic! Back at the beginning again each time, but now I have some more input that may or may not help me in the long run.

Strike three.

I kept all this mental, emotional crap, and did not deal with it. Volumes of books, magazines, online searches, religious classes, college classes, and online courses; oh, my fucking god I cannot quantify how much money, time, and energy I spent on this endeavor. Do not be like me, reader, get this book now and save yourself some hell and years.

Did you know that when you do not deal with your past bullshit, it just lowers your energy further? [iv] Great, now I am worse off than when I began, and with no answers. Yuck. I am out of ideas, people to ask, and nowhere else to turn. I am the soggy, wet logged grass fields in the middle of a thunderstorm. The water is rising, and I am being overcome, with no one to save me, and nothing I can do to stop drowning.

Fuck my life at this particular moment.

Finally, I snap. It is not necessarily a psychotic break, but it is more a gentle twig snap under your feet. I stop trying. I am just, done. Like "done-done." A fairly serious ennui has floated in. I am here at this stage for about three years. Nothing is fun anymore, and I feel nothing. I do not care about anything except my kids. I cannot even dislike something because that requires energy and emotional input. I am neutral. I have no opinion. I am nothing. I am just breathing and surviving. Even eating food becomes a chore. That sucked the worst (pre-COVID losing the sense of smell and taste) because I normally love food.

Nothing matters. I give every bit of good energy I can muster to my children. I pretend I am fine with everyone. The kids know, but do not say anything, their curious looks are met with a smile. I am just floating around waiting to sink.

After what seems like an eternity, I start to feel something. It is utterly unfamiliar.

What is this feeling?

It seems like a type of desperate last gasp of self-preservation. I do not even care what it is. It is just nice to feel something, albeit weakly. Weeks pass, and as I am waking up after yet another restless night of sleep, it hits.

In the movies when you see someone figure out the long equation that has been stumping academics for years, they are on the chalkboard all furiously writing the answer. [v]

It was like that, and all at once.

"I have to save myself?'

Long pause.

"I HAVE TO SAVE MYSELF!"

Pause again.

"Wait, what? I have to save myself. What the fuck does that even mean?"

Silence.

"Oh no, you do not mean me. Do you mean, like me, the worm, the dirt on your shoe feeling person, me? Are you serious right now?"

Silence.

"Fucking-a."

The internal thought train continues, unstoppable now, "Wait, I am supposed to stop running, and stop chasing? Really? Why?"

Well, you have the answers.

"Really? How is that? I know this is weird, that's about it."

You have always had the answers.

This dialogue started to make more sense the longer it continued. The entire internal conversation lasted two minutes and it was rapid-fire.

Those questions you asked hundreds of people - You had the answers all along. The answer to all your questions can be answered. All you have to do is stop trying to find the answer. Then the answer will appear.

"Honestly, that sounded like an asshole answer. Ok, well, now what?"

You have to make it stop.

I was beyond annoyed, readers. I took a few moments to try and wrap my head around those thoughts and answer bubbles. I realized in that moment that I am also clearly defeated by this internal realization. I acquiesce and bow my head, and cry for a few minutes. It is then I officially resigned as the one grappling inside her cocoon. Me, trying desperately to live and not succeeding very well, has hit the end of the line.

The instant internal dialogue gives me a strange aura of peace. It was perfect timing as I had exhausted literally and literarily all the resources. I had finished the entirety of the self-help section at the library. My bookcases were overflowing with religious, psychological volumes of pages - I still had gotten no answers. Then somehow this well-reasoned and perfectly timed, two-minute question and answer sequence show up.

I realize I have lived and accepted a chaotic state of being for many years, all the while in my search for answers. I am tucked deeply inside my cocoon, and I am afraid. I have run across the world and still everything follows me. A decision is made, right then. I want off of this crazy, hybrid, fucked up merry-go-round. I want it to stop. This ethereal, internal pull is graciously grabbing me by my hands and gently standing me up.

Oh, don't think I still didn't protest a bit though. Completely whooped and I still won't lay down my armor. Is it the German, the Irish, the English, or the Aries in me? More minutes pass, allowing the feeling of complete calm to expand. I finally let it all sink in.

The dialogue gives me the last bit of information, after accepting it. I know what to do.

"**I HAVE TO MAKE IT STOP**? That sounds like work."

Silence.

"Fucking-a."

The Amalgamation

Here below lies an amalgamation of all the research, reading, internal grapples, and question and answer ceremonies I have held.

It is coming in hot.

Step 1. You have to sit with it. [vi]

Start with a list.

In one of my many jobs, I worked at a weight loss clinic. Having to write down what you eat in a day, in a week, in a month, is really hard to do at first. Facing what you ingest? Ugh, it's a big deal. With this simple tool at my disposal, I had never done a serious inventory of my life; I started to write down all the things I disliked about my life. Starting with the more obvious emotional state of ennui, to my finances, and then my job. Minor and major items - I just wrote an alphabetized list (or however you choose to formulate). Obviously there are things that you cannot change, wisdom is knowing the difference of what you can and cannot. [vii]

Hard days. I loathed seeing in the physical form, clear writing, all the things that were not going my way. Coincidently... they were the things I wanted desperately to change. It was a lengthy fucking list. Then once completed, I re-read it, and put it away. Not going to lie, it hurts to see it, and it will gnaw at you too, but just do it.

Facing it all felt incredibly daunting and made me even more bummed out for a solid three days. Dear reader, once you do your list, you will feel better after a bit of time. [viii] The list of contemplations allows for the spaces of healing to begin. For once we know what we must change, then we can actually change it. Mental to physical, a manifestation of reality from our mind churnings. It is number one in my steps for a reason.

Make your list, read it, and then put it somewhere safe from prying eyes. Then, go right back to your daily life. Let the list exist. Do not keep looking at it. Only add more items if you need to. The point is to see what needs to change, and then just allow well-being and betterment to reveal themselves. Days will pass with nothing. Then, flashes of understanding and comfort will envelop you. Healing truly begins by seeing what needs to be healed. It sounds simple and too easy. Do not dismiss this step. Be brave and write your list.

Think of when you have a mosquito bite, it itches like crazy at first. You slap it, then you put itch cream on it, and you forget about it until the itch cream wears off and you feel it again. Items on your list can heal just like mosquito bites except for the timetable. That timetable is entirely up to you and your healing and how deep it is. Out of nowhere, it is all healed up, and only a tiny red dot remains of the whole bite / incident.

Other times the healing feels like when you get an accidental deep cut with purple bruising around it. It hurts every time you move that body part. Sometimes it hurts to breathe. You get stitches for really deep ones, for others you get antibiotics, and it is gone in five days. All dependent on the severity of your pain and the depth of your pain, is your complete healing after those types of emotional or otherwise - wounds. There are times it felt like there was a hole in the middle of my body and every gust of wind could just pass through it. Empty, sad, and hurt, other times it felt like that annoying itchy bite. Marinating in that fucking sadness for a hot minute, is gross.

Feel the healing.

Yes, let the mind and body restore itself. You may cry. You may be really angry and want to kick things. You may want to rip the Band-Aid[ix] off and rawdog the pain in real time. Whatever you choose to do, commit and do it. Hang in there. The more open to the mending and allowing the process to unfold organically; the more complete your healing will be. This is what people refer to as the dark night of the soul. [x] Good news though, reader, after every night is blessed daytime. Sunshine always follows the rain.

Being on the other side of traumatic shit, I can tell you, this healed and healthy side is amazing. No one told me how beautiful it is over here! Not many people I knew could explain what "this" was, because they were already here (fuck you, kindly) or they had not made it here yet. For all the beings still trapped in their turmoil, **I love you**. You can do it. I got you. We got you. We are going to be fine.

You will be ok.

How will you be ok when you feel so unbearably weak? You will because you are not just drawing on the strength of yourself, you are drawing on the people that love you. You are taking the curative energy of the Self, itself. [xi] Ancient warriors, goddesses, lords, farmers, and everyone in your lineage, and every piece of your DNA holds someone who has fought for something or against something. They are all with you. [xii] Far out, right?

It is pretty marvelous to realize your internal compass and strength.[xiii] Be kind to yourself during this healing time. See yourself with compassion. It is ok to kick yourself a bit about regrets or anything that you look back on and wish you could have managed better. You are human. Mistakes will happen. It is ok. We are human and not always our best selves at all times. Give yourself room and some emotional space to breathe.

Allowing the soothing medicine of slow or quick healing is important. Because, if you do not heal, it actually will harm you further. Letting terrible things fester inside of you then creates future harm. Issues with insomnia, indigestion, heart palpitations, or worse. It screws with your energy and frequency.[xiv] During your improvements, <u>do not</u> make worse choices (if that is even possible, I know, hard to imagine). Going out and drinking to the point of drunkenness, then climbing back into the car, and driving home, may feel good at the time. However, it does not help your healing if you get hurt or harm others. Bad decisions become like a goddamned snowball rolling down the hill snatching everything good in your life with it. Before you know it everything else in your life is snarled up into a giant thirteen-foot mass of solid, compacted, bullshit.

Own the fact that your bullshit will eventually catch up with you. It may not be soon, it could be years from now, but it will and when it does it will squash you, and anyone else you love in its vicinity. During your healing time, because you are consciously choosing to heal, your poor choices *can have a faster response time. Karma? Or is it from your self-knowing exactly what the self needs, and if you choose the other way, it smacks you back into submission?[xv] I am an idiot and got smacked around a lot from life and my choices. Do not be like me.

What I can tell you is that choosing what is right for you can be hard to understand or actually complete. The right thing is overall the best and the most beneficial. Be smart and make the right choices for yourself so you do not have to fuck around and find out. Or be dumb and a fuck up. The Universe has a way of course correction that is supremely benevolent even in the face of your extreme screwups.

Keep going in the direction of healing. Allow the healing and face your list.

The ride can be bumpy, just hold on.

Chapter 2.0

Great, now you have felt it. Sat in it for a while. It sucks, but each day it sucks a little less.

One day you feel better, and suddenly you just feel fine. Then you feel the feeling of healing and it is complete. You look at your list, and all the things you listed now seem like history. Reading it does not feel painful, instead you feel just a sense of these items as past history. WHEW! Your rumination time is over. This is a freedom you deserve, friend.

Step 2. Actions of a superhero saving themselves.[xvi]

It is all gone. Let everything you wrote down, go. Everything you felt, everything you cried through, everything you mentally battled figuratively everything. Every tiny speck of shame, guilt, anger, frustration, embarrassment, and hurt. Drop it. All of it. Baggage, luggage, purse, fanny pack, bum pack, clutch, backpack, bookbag, or whatever you mentally have been carrying all your bad shit in. Set it all down and walk away from it.

I encourage you to burn the list. Also burn anything else, non-living, like those old love letters in an outside firepit. A campfire or any outside allowable fire is encouraged. Please do not start a fire in the garage in a trashcan. Once you have burned the list, it is time to also let go of anything that ties you to the people, places, or things that were on the list that you cannot have around your space anymore. Donate the clothes, purses, items they gave to you for presents that now fill you will sadness every time you see them. Pawn or sell the jewelry they bought you. Sell the house. Trade in the car or truck. Just do not do anything illegal, friends, I know it is hard to place this on your new freedoms, but jailtime is highly discouraged. Be smart about it. It is best not to scatter all their belongings out the window of the car. That is not very tree hugger or environmentally friendly.

The freedoms you feel will overwhelm your senses for a while, and it is glorious. Revel in that beauty and majesty.

If the picture(s) you took of the event are in hardcopies or online in the cloud - decide whether you want them to exist. They can be deleted. In fact, you can delete their phone number or if you have to be in contact with them, you can change their name to something else funny. You can cut out their faces from photos or digitally crop them out of pictures. Super fun when you are ready to do so. You can block them on social media. Take them to court or tell a police officer or tell a trusted friend and tell everyone what they did or said to you. Tell their friends or tell your kids what happened.

You can get a restraining order. You can collect damages, divorce them, or whatever it is you need to do to. You can get counseling, you can join a group, you can take prescribed medications, and you can do whatever you need to. This step two is to **Act**.

Do not let old you and those choices, be the new you and your current choices.

Deal with the situation, deal with the emotions, then calmly act when it has been enough time.

"It's a bold strategy, Cotton. Let's see if it pays off for 'em."- Pepper Brooks[xvii]

The simple act of standing up and showering, after you have been sitting in your own filth for a week, have a bladder infection from not drinking anything but beer, crying for days, and not eating anything except for crackers, while chain smoking out the window of the apartment, whilst lying on the floor unable to mentally move for hours = is supremely brave and bold.

You can do it.

Moving into the action stage, is brave. I know people who refuse to deal with their emotions (formerly me) or their responsibility. Their refusal to deal with things that are ten years past, twenty, and thirty or more years gone, with the people who were involved no longer living, is maddening to watch. They keep shit they have been carrying for no other reason than they are used to feeling bad and used to the feeling of disease, chaos, the merry-go-round of badness.

They are stuck emotionally, and their bodies and other relationships in their lives are flimsy at best. Their refusal to move on or inability to, will be their downfall. That is not screwed up challenge to try this out for yourself. It will harm you the longer you keep it. This is a fact.

Time to act.

Go.

New Me Who Dis

People like to say things like "what is meant for you will stay". I say, people change. Love changes and fluctuates. Circumstances change, health, jobs, stressors, hormones change, and things can pop out of the lid when you least expect it. Unexpected pressures and fissures in your world can show up, and make you make decisions on things you were not ready for. Shit happens. You go for a quick jog and a dog leaps out at you. You go for a drive to the grocery store and a fire breaks out from under the hood of your vehicle. You go to work and come home to find your mate sexting with their ex-wife, or when you go looking for a piece of paper and find printouts of suggestive, very recent emails to their ex (low tech, but cheating is cheating).

Your new land-legs and firm foundation of healing can feel wavy at first. You are used to having sea-legs because everything up to this point has been super rough seas. The new and improved you has to stand firm emotionally, physically, spiritually, and financially. Know this, people will try you and situations will show up and expect the old you to be there. She, he, they are long gone. New you has to be strong enough to carry you, energetically, to your next level.

Step 3. Keep standing in power and standing up.

Take care of your own emotional balance and your shit. It can be large, small, or medium sized, but you need to take care of it. Be forcefully protective of your newly healed body, mind, spirit, and finances. It is healed, completely. No need to ever mention, think about, or analyze it any more than you already have.

You are whole.

New you will not mess with that old version. New you does not talk to that group anymore because they are sketchy anyways. New you does not believe in that bullshit anymore and is going to distance yourself from anything even looking like it might be a problem. Those Spanish Novellas on television are great, our talk shows, and daytime dramas are fantastic escapism. The real-life episodes of tragic events are entertaining9. But this is all just to escape your real life. Real life is weird, and humans are weird. New you is turning towards you, now, not the drama.

It will seem heartless. People will not understand the new you. They will ask, challenge, question, and even be offended by the new you. Old you would never speak in that tone. Old you would never have said things like that, in that way. Old you would have taken a different route home. New you does not care what anyone else thinks. If they do not love the new you, that is ok. Fuck 'em. New you worked through so much baggage and hardship. Old you cried at night, and slugged through life for days, months, years to get to the new you. You are never going to give up on your new you.

You have to be near militant to keep new you. New you is fresh, and clean, and diamond hard underneath. People like shiny things and they can mess with others who seem to have it figured out. Especially targeting those who are energetically higher than them.[xviii] Even worse, some people like to drag other people down just for fun.

If you have a Narcissistic mate or parent, you already know this is their entertainment for the event or evening.[xix]

How do you react? You just smile, thank them for the evening, and grab your coat, purse or wallet, and keys = and walk right out the door. Do not explain. Do not argue. Do not complain. Do not stop and turn around to respond to anything they are saying. These words from people you loved, or love may come out as nasty, horrible things. They may be things you were previously scared to hear about. Words from the pit of hell, and you cannot believe that person would dare say. Say nothing. Retreat.

You are not in a war with them, you have already won, friend. Find your peace, go for a walk, go for a cup of coffee, go to another country, just go. New you is all about peace now. If you just have two legs and your coat on, that is ok. Run if they follow you. Drive away if they threaten you. Call the authorities if they harm or attempt to harm you. New you is standing the fuck up.

Stand UP.

Look at you! All powerful, calm, and peaceful. **Celebrate that.** You are free! You are renewed, you are healed, you are sporting new energy, you are strong, and you are wonderful.

Relish the quiet. Oh, I know. It feels odd at first. Stepping off of the merry-go-round onto firm land can make you feel wobbly. Take the time to rest.

Step 4. Move along with the flow of your new, shiny self.

You will be shocked at how boring things get, really quick.

You have been warned.

Just like when you cut out all the bad parts of a moldy piece of bread, you have done this to your life. You may have to toss that piece of your life to the birds or the trash. Do it if it means keeping your peace. Healed new you doesn't want moldy bread pieces in their life and will not accept anyone else's moldy bread.

Boss not paying new you enough? Revamp your resume and start job searches. Old you's car is a shitbox? Sell it, scrap it, walk, take the bus, take a rideshare, get a friend to drive you for a few dollars, grab a taxi, or give it back to the owner. See how many doors and opportunities open when you let go of the crummy version of life you once held! It is nothing but miraculous.

The new you has opened doors to new everything as well. Whatever you want or need to have happen, in time, will happen. Think and remain positive while this transition is going on. Growing pains, if you remember them, can and will arise. There will be dark and gloomy and hard days. Others will be like sunshine and lollipops. The shark has entered the chat! You are not afraid anymore and are healed up and strong. Underlying your being will be an emanating peace and calm. It can be fun and also hard to watch everyone else on their completely disordered and confused merry-go-round.

All-in-all the good happenings, new wholesome friends, all things happy, peaceful, and healthy come along and will replace your vomit-inducing old life. Keep at it and do not step back onto that ride. Do not even look at that ride, do not touch it, do not miss it, do not have anything do to with that part of you that you have healed. Put the effort now into new you, old you had enough time to exist and needed an upgrade.

YOU WILL BE TEMPTED.

It is hard to say "no" to this charming old you behavior. Old-time thoughts, patterns of emotion, and destruction will materialize.

Step 5. Keep your peace.

I know it is dull. Your old crew is out having a fun time. On your social media those people who you thought would never not be a part of your life, are now going on about their lives while you sit watching reruns of series you have seen at least twice already. It looks like fun. Holy shit your YOLO alarm will be going off. Surprised, angry, frustrated, bored, mad, sad, depressed, you will go through these at varying times and durations. Keep hold of the new you, you are worth fighting for!

Ignore that. Ignore all of that. They are still the same. They have not put in the work you have to be new and amazing. Those toxic ones will love to see you, and then stab you in the back and go right about their days like nothing happened. If they cared, if they really missed you then they would call. They would text you to find out how you are doing. They would take you out to lunch and ask you why you have been so different lately. They will make even the tiniest bit of effort.

You want to assess to see who is down for the real you, new you, or who is just a passing acquaintance? The quickest way is to have nothing. By nothing, I mean have nothing going on, have nothing to do, have no plans, not go along with them for any reason. The second way is to make it difficult to find you. Shut down your social media pages for a month or two. Change your phone number to something no one has. Hide on purpose. See who looks for you and who does not.

It is outrageously telling to see who could care less, and who actually notices you have dropped off. I went off of all social media for years. With sincere honesty and heartbreak = only three people of the thousands of "friends" reached out. Three. They asked my brother, or asked a family member for my new number, called, texted, and actually were missing me. Fucking, three. OOOOH, that burned, readers! I was shocked, and so hurt. However, it made going into the new me era so much easier to know who was down for me and who could not give a rat's ass. I deleted numbers and I blocked people. I wanted the new me to have a chance to be 100% the real new me without anyone fake interfering.

While I fucking disappeared, I just worked and lived my most normal life. The new me was going to wait for true, and real friends. Not those people who pretended or were just acquaintances that I had made into main characters that did not deserve to be main characters.

You are the main character now.

Chapter 3.0

The results of new me were perfectly surprising, even to me at times. I took on a new name, life, outlook, lost some pounds, quit smoking (again), quit drinking so much, quit being so addicted to shopping or whatever the flavor of the month was for my old self to self-soothe by. I stopped my unending cycle of self-sabotages, got another degree, got come certificates of learnings, nice sports car, traded in the sports car for something cheaper, lived within my means, worked over one-hundred jobs (it is true, do not tell my boss). I climbed the corporate ladder, took vacations, and watched my children become adults.

Things are pretty great from where I sit today.

I am not the same person I was last year, last decade, or from my childhood. I retain most physical traits and characteristics, of course. On the whole, I am not anything like the old her. I love the new me. Old me was ok at times, but mostly flawed, could be poisonous, and incited bad energy. I personally, had to change everything entirely on my insides and break out of my cocoon. For my own sake and sanity.

What I am stepping you through is not instantaneous enlightenment. This could happen, and does happen, so no shame.

Mostly it feels like when you are making scrambled eggs, but internally. You have to be willing to look at yourself and crack yourself wide open. Pour out all the contents, take out the little bits of shell that need to be extracted from the mixing bowl or griddle. Those pieces of eggshell that over time had infiltrated you and had made it inedible if left in there. Once you have extracted the bad pieces, you mix it together with a fork (willpower, strength), air, sunshine, and light. Finally with heat (dark times), and a spatula (self-control) to keep it moving and from burning; you end up with the fluffiest, best eggs (New You) and it is tasty (better life).

My path, will thank heavens, is not your path. You did not want my path. I do not want your path. Buddhists believe there are many pathways to betterment.[xx] Just the same, I have been through enough and know enough about life to be able to show you this potential way through to a superior new you. This is hard to read and even harder to execute. For the Skeptics, I expect you lot to show up. I love people who challenge something someone tells them. Your critical thinking skills are on point. Do it.

Keep asking questions and if you do not like the answers, keep going. You, the reader, may think this is all bullshit. If this book does not resonate with you at all, no problem. If this all feels like a performative self-help book, no problem, that is OK. Pass this book onto someone else. You already paid for it. No harm, no foul. What is good for you may not be good for me. It does not bother me at all. In fact, thank you for choosing to read this far into the book and keeping up. As mentioned in the beginning of this book please toss into your donate pile for someone else to read. Whatever sticks, sticks, what is beneficial will grow in time, what is not for you, will not be for you.

The book could just be the beginning of a tiny origin story of how you got to be where you are - tomorrow. I offer you all my love, personal insight, support, hope, and the pledge of future healing. Take the steps, one-by-one, I promise if nothing else, you will gain a sense of self-awareness not had before. It takes time, which I hate to say, because I hate having to wait for anything. But it does. That stupid saying that "Time heals all" is mostly true.[xxi] The course for you is laid out. You have to do all the work.

You have to be miserable, uncomfortable, and feel like ass.

My aim in authoring this book is to simply encourage one person in their plague of a life (self-caused or otherwise) to recreate themselves. We cannot just change our clothes and find everything is magically fixed. I have tried that. It feels great but is noticeably short in its lasting power. Also, it is expensive. No, we must do the inward changes first, then work our way outward.

If you are taking the steps and still hanging on and ready to move forward, then you are ready for the next step.

Step 6. You get to create your new life.

The new you is limitless potential.

You have survived the soul crushing nights, gotten firm in your foundation of yourself, and have seen who is real and who is fake. You have done advanced level emotional, spiritual, financial, and physical shit. You are on the next level. It is time to get creative.

Your mind is remarkable. You singularly have the power to change your mind. You can do anything to learn or substitute old mental pathways and data.[xxii] The giant sponge that is your brain is ready to be hardwired for success. Victory for you can mean anything from being able to say no to that second plate of dessert, to not buying that pack of cigarettes, or not taking shitty behavior from your partner anymore.

How does one reroute old, familiar pathways? Those knee jerk reactions we have to stimulus; how do we stop instantly becoming pissed off or hurt or angry or whatever?

We hardwire it in.

Upsides

Flipping the Script is a tool for writers from songwriters to mystery writers.[xxiii] When you find yourself in a conversation or situation that old you would normally react a certain way to that you are not implementing into the new you, you do a proper Reverse Uno.[xxiv] You dead-on do the opposite of what they anticipate you will do. Laughing instead of crying also works, as well as a thumbs up or thumbs down instead of talking back to the person, all are valid replies. This is actually one of my favorite things to do. Keeping a straight face while they sit there stunned, actually is quite entertaining. Not yelling, not getting angry, not being embarrassed, not shooting nasty words back at them, not whatever it is, is beautiful.

The power!

The unexpected calm and quiet answer to their line-of-fire questioning is outright precious. My face might blush from the rush of emotions I am feeling, but I do not act out. I pause, mentally count to ten, think about what I am going to say next, and in a lowered and firm tone - I reply.

This takes practice, friend. Especially with Narcissists, those gd assholes will trigger you at the slightest movement. Be calm inside of you, be calm in your head, and be calm in your voice as best you can. You win. You already won by not yelling back at them. They will get even more bothered by your temperate speech. Let them rage and spin out of control, let them. Fuck 'em. Let them spew hate chunks from their lips. Let them whirl into a tornado of badness and let them reach heights of inappropriate behavior unseen by most humans.

You get the fuck out of there if they get handsy at all or explosive to the point of violence.[xxv] Either way, you remain even, calm, and neutral even if you do not feel like it. Then, once they have reached a point where you are done with the whole thing: you calmly (act if you have to) grab your coat, keys, wallet, and you walk slowly out the fucking door. No rabid chipmunks for you, no moldy bread behavior, no old you stormy bullshit = new you does not take any of that brutal behavior, words, or deeds from anyone.

This will splinter stormy relationships, and <u>that is ok.</u> Let them splinter and crack. New you is not here for any type of verbal/physical/emotional/spiritual/financial abuse, neglect, being ignored, not being respected, not being listened to, and not standing here being someone who gets savage behaviors from someone who has not done the work to work on themselves and instead uses you as a punching bag. Yes, old you put up with seriously contentious shit.

New you does not play with any of that crap anymore.

The given steps can be repeated and/or circling on a step is fine. When it is time to move onto the next one, you will know, and you will do it sometimes subconsciously. Your timeline, is your timeline. If you need someone to assist you at any time you are taking these steps, please reach out to someone you trust, or a professional. Renovations take time and energy, just like the rest of this does. Again, the jackpot of doing all that internal work on yourself to make yourself renewed is the brand new you. This new you has the distinction of being a higher level being, overcoming obstacles, and on a premium path to betterment.

Doing the Script Flip is one way to rewire. It works. Another way to hardwire new you is to sit in silence for a few moments during your day. Any time of day is fine. I like to do this before I get up for the day, or when I plan my day out before heading into the shower. Many people like to pray, meditate, read a book, sit in front of a window, or some lay in bed and think of all the things to be grateful for the day ahead.[xxvi] No electronics, no music, no nothing - just you and your thoughts. You have done this before while working on your list. You did this again when you spent time feeling the feelings. This time it is more about just being, not doing.

Now daily, one minute at first, then stretch it to five, then add more time if you like. Set an alarm so that you are not looking at the time, the whole time. Sit down with a cup of coffee, tea, orange juice, water, and just gaze out the window. Stand up or sit on the balcony, or the deck. Purposefully have nothing to do besides think positive thoughts, or no thoughts if you can muster that. I am never able not to think, so I just let whatever floats up, just be there. Or you can use this little time to manifest.[xxvii]

You can use this time to quiet your anxiety about work. You can use this time to just get Vitamin D from the sunshine. You can use this time to not have anyone demanding of your time, and just be quiet. Use this time and do this **daily**. It feels a little weird at first, your mind may fight back a bit too because it is used to constant stimulus. That is ok. Let it wear itself out. Eventually you will be able to just sit and Be.

Do not judge your thoughts, let them run amok.[xxviii] Mantras are fantastic if you cannot think of anything to do right away.[xxix] Singing to yourself or aloud and proudly also has benefits if you are in a space for that. Humming works just as well. Basically, find what works for you and do it daily and repeat it without stopping for as long as you can. I broke my 185-day record because I got lazy one morning and forgot to have this simple time-out time for myself. My mental health that day I skipped my time, was less than stellar. The habit is so good, you will want to keep doing this for as long as you live.

This is a wonderful habit, treasure this time for you, new you.

Glowing in the Night

Once you get your personal time schedule and pattern it into your daily life - you will see changes in your life. They are part of the hardwire. New you loves it. You do not have to explain your process or progress to anyone if you do not want to. Sometimes being private and working on ourselves is a solitary effort and should not be a conversation topic until you are ready and healed. Just share with a good person when you are ready. Bringing yourself into awareness, grounding, centering, or whatever you deem is what you can do for yourself that brings about more serenity into your busy life = is the goal.[xxx] Flipping the script and slowing down your mind and heart rate will create bonus health points as well.

Just start.

I am a yoga teacher. Most days I have to force myself to do yoga asanas (the physical portion of yoga). Physical activity is not my usual state since I was in my 20s. How does one instruct and practice, yet dislike to practice? I know it is good for me. I know it helps me. It has assisted in helping me shed over one-hundred and twenty pounds over the years, keeps my back flexible after sitting in a chair all day, and my body loves it. Once I start, I am always happy, it's just the start. Which is like everything in life, hard for a quick moment then it becomes easier.

The literal millisecond I get out of bed before anything else (besides using the toilet) every morning I get on the floor or onto my mat. I keep my mat under my bed or will have a towel handy, or just plop right down on a small, cleaner section of the carpet or floor. I do this so my mind does not have the chance to rebel or talk me out of it. Daily, practice, and habit; get comfortable with these words and their meanings. Would you think drinking more water and hitting the mat every morning for six months, doing only five minutes of yoga will give you a sixpack? It can! If you do it right and do this daily you will be very surprised how everything about you feels just a bit healthier and better. Chair yoga, wheelchair yoga, bed yoga, floor yoga, whatever you can do physically, daily, the results will show up.

Do what works for you.

Add extended time for your self-time, anything physical will do, if you can. Do something that moves your body. If you just cannot that day, do something mental like mantras, reading a good self-help book (hint), or meditation. Movement time can be spent taking a walk, taking the pet for a walk, using the treadmill, doing the dishes, or cleaning up after the family. Take your time daily, every day, try for streak like I do or whatever can do to prepare to make this successfully a habit. Set an alarm for this me time so you are not distracted by the clock.

<u>An example:</u>

1. Lay in bed for two minutes and think positive thoughts about the upcoming day ahead

2. Get on the floor and do five minutes of yoga

3. Read five to twenty minutes of a book

-OR-

1. Before going to sleep, think about all the good things that happened during your day

2. Once you wake up, sit up, and stretch your limbs for five minutes

3. Sit and meditate, pray, or say a mantra for ten minutes

Bundle how it works for you and for the optimal time of day. Keep in mind your activity and level of energy. Just do it, daily! I know, I am so annoying about this, but I mean it. People do things like keep track on their email calendars or write down a check mark next to a to-do list that has "Me-Time" listed. Whatever is clever.

The rewired new you needs to have new things to do.

Keep honoring the new you.

There are so many advantages of grounding time, or your daily self-time that I cannot list them all in this little book.[xxxi]

Here are the items that can *potentially* come from your daily you-time:

- boosted confidence
- lowered stress levels
- better skin health due to lowered stress levels
- emotional health increased
- mood enhanced
- firmer muscles, due to increased gentle movements
- lost weight due to regular movement
- less cravings for sugary and salty foods, and snacks
- lowered psychological illness impact of previously triggering events
- more restful sleep
- answers to questions you have had and were not quiet enough to hear because you kept yourself so busy and distracted
- full glow ups
- transcendence

- getting closer to You, your Being, Essence, the True Self, or God
- ego death
- magnanimity
- increased speed and communication within your cells
- inspiration to do, write, sing, say, or complete something you've been putting off
- behavioral changes for the better
- clearer thinking and recall times
- not starting off the day or ending your day all freaked out and stressed and anxious for once
- attractions for manifesting increase

If you receive any one of these items I will be incredibly happy for you.

You may even have a type of bundle show up all at once.

You might not have any show up for a minute.

That is ok.

Let us just follow this through all the way so you can see what new *potential you can look forward to. Tomorrow you start meditating with a meditation app on your phone every morning on your commute to work. Your stress levels decrease because you are beginning your usually super-stressful workday now at ease and less anxious. You start doing better at your job because you are not stressed out all the time. You incorporate a manifesting time into your you-time in the morning before you leave for work. Your manifesting and meditation time pay off. A few months later you get a raise, a bonus, or a promotion. Yes, that is correct, your fifteen minutes a day turned into $2000.00 USD in this scenario.

Results may vary. For me: I have lost over 133 pounds over the years (at time of publication), doing low-impact yoga. I did slow, relaxing yoga. Obviously, I am going to plug yoga. Yoga works and has for thousands of years. It has done such amazing things for me that I am forever a supporter of those willing to try it.

I started out doing one hour a day while the kids were asleep for their naps. Right after I was cleared to exercise after the six weeks post-delivery, I bought a video and got to work. At first, I cried a lot. I was not flexible. I was moody from hormones, and I was miserable. I could not reach my toes. I cried because I thought I would never get my pre-pregnancy body back to even close to what my body was before. I was depressed for a while, but I kept at it. The day I could reach my toes -I stopped crying. I began to see some weight loss; things were firming up. What was this strange happening? Yoga was working. I was hooked! The kids are adults now. The results have been nothing short of incredible for me.

You time, daily, do it, and some yoga.

Chapter 4.0

Hey, look at you go, go You!!!!!

All the hard work is paying off and you are seeing, feeling, behaving, sleeping, eating, legitimately everything is gradually or all-at-once better. You are on the other side of your old bullshit. Nine days out of ten you are a little bored, have a routine, and also are calm. The triggers are not that triggering. The toxic people and situations have all but ceased to exist in your life. Sure, you have the odd one-off day which does not seem to go your way. Overall, though, you are an overcoming being living in a sea of badassery.

There will be times, days, weeks when you overindulge in food or drinks. Treat yourself. This is meant to help you. Medium way is the best way, folks. [xxxii] If it turns into something that controls your life, then it is time to see someone or start talking to someone to assist that is a specialist in that area. Overall, though, the life you are leading is nothing less than exceptional.

YOU DID THIS!

You too have lived a thousand lifetimes in the last few days, months, and years and now are reaping the rewards of said arduous work. Now what? Depending on who you talk to or read up on, chaos is our usual state, or chaos is an unnatural state of being.[xxxiii] I prefer to think chaos to be contained and transmuted within ourselves, personally. Once we do these steps, the chaos grinds down to a tiny speck. It still exists in us, however; it does not ignite easily and stays small for as long as we keep it small. Can we control everything around us? No. Can we control other people, no. We can control how we react, how we behave, and what we think.

Step 7. Monkey Mind is an asshole.[xxxiv]

Control your thoughts.

The best way I learned how to do this is to practice Present moment awareness.[xxxv]

This is a key which assists in your daily successes.

We have fully felt our feelings. We have dealt with all the past hurts. We have acted upon our best self to gain any or all the items or money or _______ that is owed to us because of their improper actions. We have forgiven and let it all go. We have pushed mountains of garbage back into the landfill, buried it all, and stamped the ground to mark it complete. Our thoughts, however, even with the work, breakthroughs, body work, and breathwork - can be a divisive force. The mind can retain patterns which need considerable force to disassemble.

The Immersion

Mingyur Rinpoche talks about the Monkey Mind and being presently aware of your thoughts and emotions.[xxxvi] He talks about doing the dishes. Most of us have dishwashers or do the dishes ourselves in the sink, so this one was an easy one to relate to. When you are doing the dishes, do the dishes in your head as well. Fully concentrate on only doing the dishes. Do not daydream, do not go anywhere else, do not mentally disappear to somewhere else. Think about how the water feels on your hands. Feel the suds. How heavy is the dishwashing detergent bottle when you pour it? How hot is the water? How much strength and scrubbing does it take to get that one really caked on dish, clean?

Full immersion into what you are doing. Full stop. That is present moment awareness in a nutshell. Be right in the moment. Be fully present, not thinking of past things, not thinking of future things, just being right here, right now. Practice this while eating your next meal. How does it taste? Is it too salty, is it too sweet? Does the food burn from the heat? Is it spicy or does it need something to add to it? Is it taking forever to chew through because it is too tough? Is it cold and needs to be warmed up? You do not need to ask yourself these questions. These are just suggestions to tap into the experience directly at that very second.

Once you are feeling and really into your meal, savor it. My Grammy used to say, "Savor the journey". She was a smart woman. Enjoy the process itself, not just the end result. Take in all the sights, smells, and sounds of what is around you at that very moment. Embrace the now of right now. Are you sitting in an airport waiting for your flight? Listen to the people around you, smell the food from the vendors and restaurants, and feel the marginally acceptable seat on which you are planted.

Experience your moment at that very moment.

You will get particularly good at this. Inherently, as you take in and live in the moment itself, you will start to notice those zombies around you that are just skimming the surface of life. They are buried in their phones. They are pacing the floor in frustration. They are annoyed at traffic and clausterphobic sitting there waiting for the green light. No, not you. You are not going to live on standby mode anymore. You are going to sit and enjoy your layover between flights. You grab a magazine or book, and you settle in. Or you turn on the radio and listen to Classical music to calm yourself down while stuck in traffic. Once you are feeling less annoyed, you carefully notice the buildings and how lovely a day it is outside in between breaking.

Cannot seem to get into the present moment mode? Play! Go hang out with your kids and do something creative. Go outside and make a crown with flowers. Write a book, a play, or a screenplay. Do not judge what it is, just do it. Go into any legal and healthy activity completely. It will immediately snap you into the present moment. The wonderful childlike behaviors we lose as adults is having only what is going on - right then. Are kids worried about work? No. Are they thinking about what is for dinner? No. Are they behind on laundry and if you do not do the laundry soon, no one will have clothes to wear? No. Leave all that crap for later, and just be right now in the creation.

Luke 10:38-42 in the Christian Bible talks about Jesus and the women preparing, serving, and attending their feast.[xxxvii] One woman is so intent on making sure her guests and the esteemed Jesus are comfortable and well fed, that she is actually missing the dinner party. She is missing the party! Do you get it?

You are missing life because you have not been enjoying yourself in the conversations, meals, flights, walks, workings, and any activities that have happened. Up until now, you have been absent. You were not actually "there" for any of the words you have exchanged with another person, until you practiced present moment awareness.

Holy shit, right? See what I did there?

Sit with that one for a moment.

Just like everything else in life, this present moment awareness takes practice. The next time you talk to anyone face-to-face, really look at their face, or if it is someone with which you are familiar and are blind, feel their face. Gently look or feel and "see" them for the first time. The mole on their cheek, the freckle on their nose, the arch of their eyebrows, the present moment awareness extends to people very well. Notice their tone of voice or feel the skin of their hands in your hand. The immersion into this practice is immediate and worth it.

Pardon the cliche, but awareness really does make food taste better. I know, it sounds stupid, but really it is true. Your sky is bluer, and your conscious mind becomes more under your control. Some people with mental illnesses may have more of a battle with this practice. This is ok. I battled with this for a while as well. It is good to note that we all have something wrong with us, friend. You just do your best with what you got.

Try this for one meal. Try it for one meeting. Try it for one hour during your favorite television show. Be there and be fully into it and aware. It is life changing. I promise. The more you do this, the mind becomes less like a non-stop fly, buzzing in your ear. Your mind can be trained to behave better than before, by being present. It is a superpower to be fully engaged in the world around you and with the people you deal with, and with yourself. Once I learned this skill, I have never looked back and have never turned it off. It is nothing less than unbelievable and you will want everyone around you to learn how to do it as well.

Chapter 5.0

Life is good! Your mind is running on a higher, and better frequency. Your body is working at a greater or enhanced level. Remember where you started off? Struggling to write that list, and now look at you go!!!

Your life is of a quality you had not previously had. You worked those steps. Your days are spent feeling, seeing, and experiencing life. You are no longer a chattering-brained zombie. I said what I said. You might have changed friends, or even spouses. You may have even traded in the job you hated, or you might still be at the job you hate but now after work do something fun thing that offsets the last 8-10 hours you spent at work.

Life is more fulfilling.

Bowling, soccer, tennis, yoga, writing, sewing, playing a game, joining a band, going to a live concert, going to a live sports arena to watch your favorite team, paying for a subscription online to see an event, reading a book, going to a meeting with likeminded people, going to the bar, or just changing out of your work clothes and into your comfiest pajamas and enjoying sluglife for a while. Whatever you choose, choose it for the new you.

Step 8. Choose to live your life.

Yes, it takes energy, and right now reading this might all seem too much. That is ok. When you get to this stage, it is nothing short of a good time. I want what is best for you. You have responsibilities, work, children to deal with, vehicles to fix, and clothing to wash/dry/fold/put away. The To-Do list for everyone is endless. Choosing to be present moment for as much of your day as you can. Choose to be the best version of yourself. Even when we think we do not have a choice in the matter, there are always ways for us to participate that are healthy for us, or harmful for us.

We get to choose how we behave, act, think, and live.

Cannot leave that horrid relationship, yet? Ok. Settle in. Make those mental changes to how you react to their words or behaviors. Make a game plan in the meantime. Cannot wait until the children are off to college? You have a few more years until then, ok. Present moment with them, enjoy something about them - their laughs, their ways of seeing things and telling you about their world. Mentally notate this the next time they are making you feel crazy and/or annoyed.

In the end, these are major changes you have made.

I am so proud of you!

Final thoughts and summaries:

Let it go, all of it, just do it, seriously, do not keep that emotional war raging in you.

You have the power.

You are responsible for yourself.

You can absolutely change anything in your life that is not permanent. Most things are not permanent.

Being a better version of yourself automatically signs you up for a better life.

You are an infinite being of light or darkness, whichever you prefer.

You be the best you; you can be.

Once you learn how to be present moment, you get to choose your level of present moment awareness.

You have incredible willpower.

You have everything you have ever needed or wanted from others = already inside of you.

You have already won by trying. Most people do not try. Do not be like most people.

The work you put into making yourself the new you, is never a waste of time.

Your spirit / soul / heart is just a cultivation of your mind, your intelligence, your behavior, and your connectedness with others. You will feel more connected with everything once you put in the work on yourself. Weird but true.

Good people to keep around are those that never see you as a threat, when you are leveling up. They want you to be happy and fulfilled. Keep them close.

Get out of zombie mode and into actual living.

Change is good, emotional chaos is not great. Choose good even if chaos is a fucking tempting tempter of the highest levels.

Notes

---

[i] Koutsky, Judy. "48 Hours in Osceola, Wisconsin: Small-Town Charm with Plenty to Do." Forbes, 8 Sept. 2021, www.forbes.com/sites/judykoutsky/2021/09/08/48-hours-in-osceola-wisconsin-small-town-charm-with-plenty-to-do/?sh=172f64957d70. Accessed 20 Jan. 2024.

[ii] "Tower Graffiti." Osceolasun.com, 16 Aug. 2022, www.osceolasun.com/tower-graffiti/image_56d0ef5c-1d71-11ed-99ed-6b1d451ee908.html. Accessed 20 Jan. 2024.

[iii] "Latin Quotes by Virgil." Latin-Phrases.dechile.net, latin-phrases.dechile.net/?Virgil. Accessed 20 Jan. 2024.

[iv] Greg Gillaird. "How to Raise Your Vibration When Depressed in 5 Steps." Https://Selffulmaven.com/, 15 Sept. 2021, selffulmaven.com/2021/09/how-to-raise-your-vibration-when-depressed-and-unhappy-in-5-steps/. Accessed 20 Jan. 2024.

[v] A Beautiful Mind. Directed by Ron Howard, Film, Universal Pictures,

DreamWorks, 2001.

vi Knight, Katie. "The Uncomfortable Art of Sitting with Yourself." Medium, 4 Feb. 2021, medium.com/p/e75bade53b11. Accessed 20 Jan. 2024.

Drew Linsalata. "EP 126 - Learning to Sit Still and Be Alone with Yourself." The Anxious Truth, 7 Oct. 2020, theanxioustruth.com/ep-126-sitting-still/. Accessed 20 Jan. 2024.

vii "Prayer for Serenity // Faith at Marquette // Marquette University." Www.marquette.edu, www.marquette.edu/faith/prayer-serenity.php#:~:text=Attributed%20to%20Reinhold%20Niebuhr%2C%20Lutheran. Accessed 20 Jan. 2024.

viii Baldwin, Jayron. "The Benefits of Writing down Your Thoughts and Feelings - the Adroit Journal." The Adroit Journal, 3 Apr. 2020, theadroitjournal.org/2020/04/03/the-benefits-of-writing-down-your-thoughts-and-feelings/#. Accessed 20 Jan. 2024. Blog.

ix "Wound Care Products: Adhesive Bandages, Wraps, Tapes & More." BAND-AID® Brand Adhesive Bandages, www.band-aid.com/products. Accessed 20 Jan. 2024.

x Gunnarson, Julie. "Eckhart on the Dark Night of the Soul | by Eckhart Tolle." Eckhart Tolle | Official Site - Spiritual Teachings and Tools for Personal Growth and Happiness, 2 Apr. 2018, eckharttolle.com/eckhart-on-the-dark-night-of-the-soul/#:~:text=It%20is%20a%20term%20used. Accessed 6 Feb. 2024.

xi Arlin Cuncic, MA . "How to Align Your Inner and Outer Self." Verywell Mind, 2019, www.verywellmind.com/tension-between-inner-self-and-outer-self-4171297.

Haymond, Bryce. "The Falling Away of Ego Consciousness in Hinduism and Buddhism." Thy Mind, O Human, 14 May 2018, www.thymindoman.com/the-falling-away-of-ego-consciousness-in-hinduism-and-buddhism/. Accessed 20 Jan. 2024.

xii Piastrelli, Becca. "How to Connect with Your Ancestral Lineage | Becca Piastrelli." Beccapiastrelli.com, beccapiastrelli.com/guide-to-ancestors/. Accessed 20 Jan. 2024.

xiii Sasson, Remez. "What Is Inner Strength and How to Develop It." Success Consciousness, 12 July 2020, www.successconsciousness.com/blog/inner-strength/how-to-develop-inner-strength/. Accessed 26 Jan. 2024.

xiv Wellman, Jodi. "The Top Six Things That Are Snuffing the Vitality out of You I Four Thousand Mondays." Four Thousand Mondays, 17 May 2021, fourthousandmondays.com/the-top-six-things-that-are-snuffing-the-vitality-out-of-you/. Accessed 26 Jan. 2024.

xv BROWN, TAYLOR. "16 People Share the Best Example of Instant Karma They've Ever Witnessed." Someecards, 30 June 2023, www.someecards.com/lifestyle/karma/16-people-share-the-best-example-of-instant-karma-theyve-ever-witnessed/. Accessed 26 Jan. 2024.

xvi Miller, Natasha. "6 Strategies to Save Yourself (instead of Waiting for a Hero)." Entrepreneur, 26 June 2022, www.entrepreneur.com/leadership/6-strategies-to-save-yourself-instead-of-waiting-for-a/428592. Accessed 26 Jan. 2024.

xvii "Dodgeball: A True Underdog Story (2004) - IMDb." Www.imdb.com, www.imdb.com/title/tt0364725/characters/nm0170550. Accessed 26 Jan. 2024.

xviii Itani, Omar. "Beware of 'the Crab Mentality': How Your Environment Can Shape the Way You Think and Behave." OMAR ITANI, 24 Oct. 2020, www.omaritani.com/blog/the-crab-mentality.

xix "Narcissistic Personality Disorder - Symptoms and Causes." Mayo Clinic, www.mayoclinic.org/diseases-conditions/narcissistic-personality-disorder/symptoms-causes/syc-20366662#:~:text=Have%20an%20inability%20or%20unwillingness.

xx Greenwood, Gesshin. "Welcome to the Ten Thousand Things." Ten Thousand Things, 16 Jan. 2020, blog.shin-ibs.edu/welcome-to-the-ten-thousand-things/. Accessed 23 Jan. 2024.

xxi Godkin, PhD, Sophia. "'Time Heals All Wounds' – Is It Really True?" Www.thehappinessdoctor.com, 7 Feb. 2023, www.thehappinessdoctor.com/blog/time-heals-all-wounds. Accessed 26 Jan. 2024.

xxii ""Changing Habits - Learning Center." Learning Center, 2019, learningcenter.unc.edu/tips-and-tools/changing-habits/. Accessed 26 Jan. 2024.

xxiii Goyer, Tiffany. "How to Singlehandedly Improve Any Relationship: Part 8, Flip the Script." Tiffany Goyer, LMFT, 9 Oct. 2020, www.tiffanygoyer.com/blog/flip-the-script. Accessed 26 Jan. 2024.

xxiv "Shop UNO." Mattel Shop, shop.mattel.com/collections/uno. Accessed 26 Jan. 2024.

xxv Smith, Melinda, and Jeanne Segal. "How to Get out of an Abusive Relationship." HelpGuide.org, 2 Nov. 2018, www.helpguide.org/articles/abuse/getting-out-of-an-abusive-relationship.htm. Accessed 26 Jan. 2024.

xxvi "How to Practice Gratitude." Mindful, 25 Nov. 2019, www.mindful.org/an-introduction-to-mindful-gratitude/. Accessed 26 Jan. 2024.

xxvii Miles, Madeline. "14 Things to Manifest in Every Area of Your Life." Www.betterup.com, 1 June 2023, www.betterup.com/blog/things-to-manifest. Accessed 26 Jan. 2024.

xxviii Carmen, Ashley. "If You Notice Thoughts during Meditation, You're Doing It Right." Wonder Therapy, 23 Mar. 2019, wondertherapy.net/thoughts-during-meditation/. Accessed 26 Jan. 2024.

[xxix] Yugay, Irina. "The Most Comprehensive Guide List of Mantras for Meditation." Mindvalley Blog, 20 May 2020, blog.mindvalley.com/mantra-meditation/. Accessed 26 Jan. 2024.

[xxx] Arzt, LMFT, Nicole. "Grounding Techniques: Examples & How They Help." Choosing Therapy, 6 Dec. 2022, www.choosingtherapy.com/grounding-techniques/. Accessed 26 Jan. 2024.

[xxxi] Woodyard, Catherine. "Exploring the Therapeutic Effects of Yoga and Its Ability to Increase Quality of Life." International Journal of Yoga, vol. 4, no. 2, Dec. 2011, pp. 49–54, https://doi.org/10.4103/0973-6131.85485.

[xxxii] Bhikku, Buddhadasa. "The Middle Way." Buddhism Now, 22 Jan. 2013, buddhismnow.com/2013/01/22/middle-way-buddhadasa-bhikkhu/. Accessed 26 Jan. 2024.

[xxxiii] Sutter , Paul. "An Unpredictable Universe: A Deep Dive into Chaos Theory." Space.com, 18 Mar. 2022, www.space.com/chaos-theory-explainer-unpredictable-systems.html. Accessed 26 Jan. 2024.

[xxxiv] "Calming the Monkey Mind: 7 Mindful Steps." Synctuition, 2 Mar. 2022, synctuition.com/blog/calming-the-monkey-mind-7-mindful-steps/. Accessed 26 Jan. 2024.

[xxxv] "Present-Moment Awareness: Overview, Benefits, and Practice." The Human Condition, 14 Oct. 2021, thehumancondition.com/present-moment-awareness/. Accessed 26 Jan. 2024.

[xxxvi] Braymiller, Ganesh. "Mingyur Rinpoche – BHNN Guest Podcast – Ep. 82 – the Neuroscience of Meditation." Be Here Now Network, 16 Aug. 2021, beherenownetwork.com/mingyur-rinpoche-bhnn-guest-podcast-ep-82-the-neuroscience-of-meditation/. Accessed 26 Jan. 2024.

[xxxvii] Holy Bible (NIV). Zondervan, 2008.

www.ingramcontent.com/pod-product-compliance
Lightning Source LLC
LaVergne TN
LVHW091238150826
845673LV00003B/1210

9798218373788